Strings in Step
violin

BOOK
TWO

Jan Dobbins

Music Department
OXFORD UNIVERSITY PRESS
Oxford and New York

TEACHERS' NOTES

Strings in Step Book 2 builds on the concepts and skills introduced in Book 1. It begins with a revision section of exercises, tunes, and a theory worksheet. The book is in six sections, each covering approximately one term's work. It contains:

1. New tunes, traditional tunes, and classical tunes.
2. All scales up to and including those for Associated Board Grade 2.
3. Careful presentation of finger patterns 0–1–23–4; 0–12–3–4; 01–2–34; 0–1–2–34.
4. Explanation of key signatures.
5. Lively ensemble pieces in C, G, and D majors which can be played in various combinations with the other stringed instruments.
6. Teaching pages for the dotted crotchet, the semiquaver, the triplet, the dotted quaver and semiquaver, and $\frac{6}{8}$ time.
7. Teaching pages for string crossing, bow recovery, double stopping, and left hand pizzicato.
8. Theory worksheets following on from those in Book 1.
9. Ideas and games to foster skill in improvising and composing.
10. The cello book contains an introduction to fourth position.

As in Book 1 practice and achievement records monitor progress and pupils are encouraged to plan their own concert performances.

Colour coding

The colour coding system introduced in Book 1 is developed to further pupils' understanding of key structure. Encourage children to colour all diagrams as follows:

First finger   – red
Second finger – yellow
Third finger   – green
Fourth finger – blue

When the scale diagrams are coloured in this way the pattern of tones and semitones becomes very clear. By colouring the diagrams as they are learned, the pupils can quickly and easily check which scales they have to practise.

Piano accompaniments ◀P▶

All tunes which have piano accompaniments are marked with the letter 'p' in the Pupil Books. The page number for the Pupil Book is given at the top of each piece in the Piano Book. Accompaniments are provided for all tunes and exercises in Book 2 with the following exceptions:

a) The rounds, which are best unaccompanied.
b) The scales.
c) The bowing exercises (Pupil Book page 22) and the double stopping exercises (Pupil Book page 25).

Ensemble playing

Ensemble playing is developed in this book through a series of trios which are graded in difficulty.

'O Come Little Children' comprises three parts of equivalent standard.

'Carol' and 'Winster Galop' have a very easy third part which can be played by pupils who are still working on Book 1. (Useful for bringing all the instrumentalists together for a concert!)

'J'irais Revoir ma Normandie' and 'Basque Song' demand more skill in ensemble playing and have parts of equivalent standard.

Use the ensemble pieces as a resource for developing orchestral skills. The pieces can be arranged in a variety of ways to produce an effective performance. For example, 'Carol' can be played as follows:

    First Time: All instruments play the tune (A)

    Second Time: Pizzicato – violins play A; violas play B; cellos play C.

    Third Time: Arco – violins play A; violas play B; cellos play C.

    Try to give pupils the opportunity to play the ensembles with one player to each part in order to develop and refine listening skills. The trios also work well as duets when two of the parts are supported by the piano accompaniment.

N.B.   Tunes or exercises which cannot be played in ensemble with the other instruments in the series are indicated by an asterisk, ✳ .

Improvisation and composition

The games and worksheets on pages 11, 35, 39, and 44 suggest ways in which improvisation and composition can be introduced and developed. They are not intended as a rigid structure. Pupils vary enormously in their ability to compose or improvise freely. Use the ideas on these pages to stimulate their interest and listen to their suggestions. These can often lead to exciting new ideas for games or the development of a group composition.

Using the book as a teaching resource

The information in Book 2 is presented in a logical order with concepts and skills reinforced at each stage. Pupils working through the material in the order in which it is presented gain a thorough understanding of technical and theoretical skills needed for Associated Board Grades 1 and 2, and some aspects of Grade 3. The improvisation, composition, and ensemble work is valuable preparation for GCSE coursework. The book can also be used as a 'bank' of ideas and teaching points when pupils are learning repertoire or examination pieces.

Jan Dobbins 1991

CONTENTS

SECTION 1

Revision Exercises

D major

A major

G major

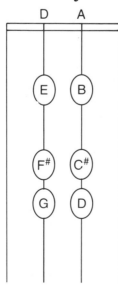

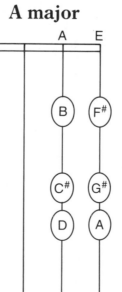

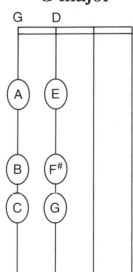

D major	A major	G major

Scale Games

D major

Play the whole scale ascending and descending in the following ways:

Try no. 3 with three players, i.e. three 'hello's' on each note. Try singing as you play!

Play the scale games with all the scales which you learn

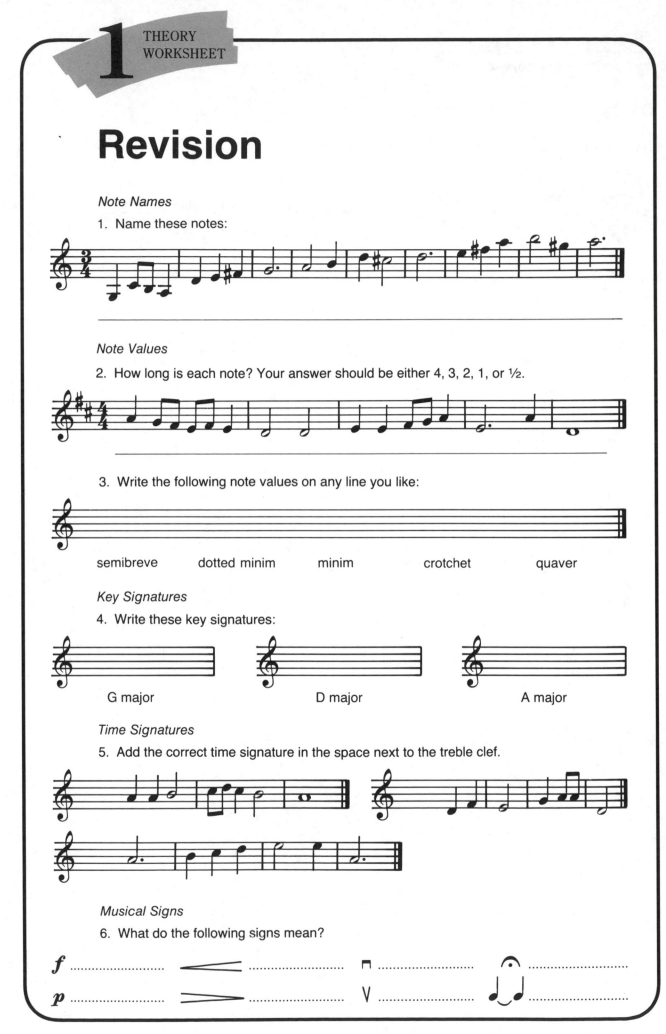

Revision

Note Names

1. Name these notes:

Note Values

2. How long is each note? Your answer should be either 4, 3, 2, 1, or ½.

3. Write the following note values on any line you like:

semibreve   dotted minim   minim   crotchet   quaver

Key Signatures

4. Write these key signatures:

G major   D major   A major

Time Signatures

5. Add the correct time signature in the space next to the treble clef.

Musical Signs

6. What do the following signs mean?

f ....

p ....

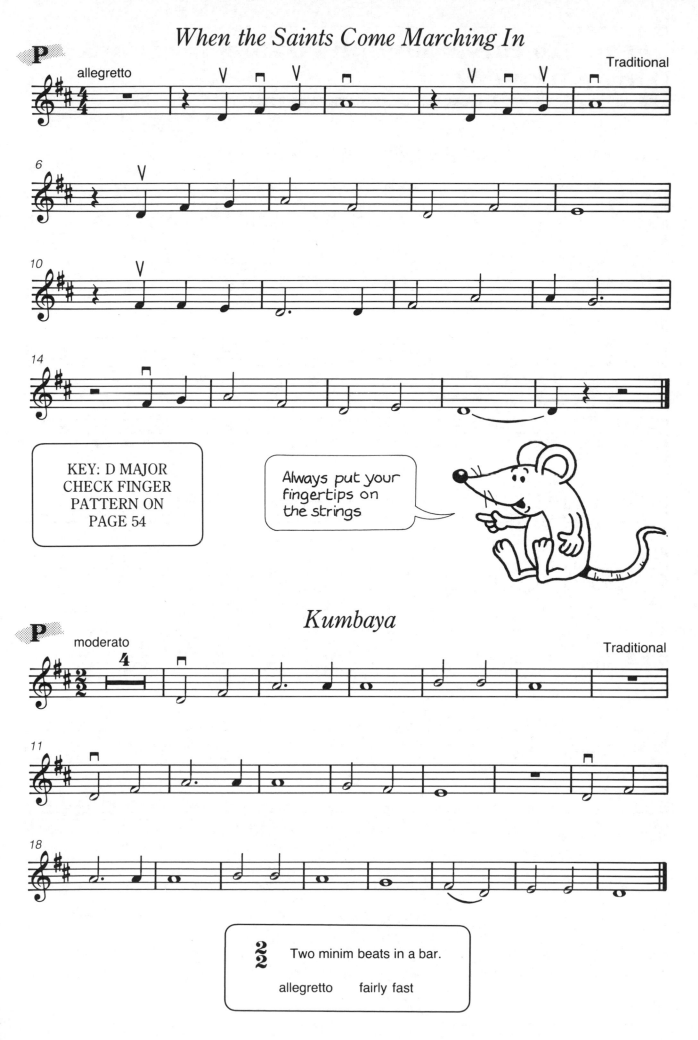

Trio. An ensemble piece for three players

O Come Little Children

Traditional

Improvisation

Answering phrases

An answering phrase is like the answer to a question.
　　Here is a question: *What is your name?*
　　The answer might be: *My name is Sam.*
Look at this tune and ask your teacher to play it to you. The first phrase is the question. The second phrase is the answer.

first phrase　　　　　　　second phrase

The answer balances the question.
Ask your teacher or a friend to play the following tunes to you and then see if you can play a phrase to finish each tune:

1.

Start your answer on A and end on D. Play any notes you like in between.

2.

Start your answer on E and end on A. Play any notes you like in between.

3.

Start your answer on D or E and end on G.

> Work with a friend and try to make up your own tune.
> Start your tune on D or A or G.

A New Position for Second Finger on the D String

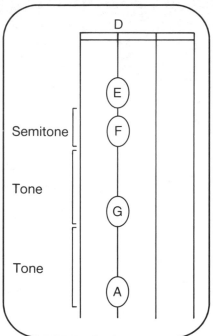

Miserable Musician

Song of the River

A New Position for Second Finger on the A String

Now try the C major scale and arpeggio on page 58.

A New Position for Second Finger on the E String

The Scale of G Major

Green Umbrellas

Now you are ready to learn the scale of G major (two octaves) on page 56.

The Natural Sign

This is the natural sign:

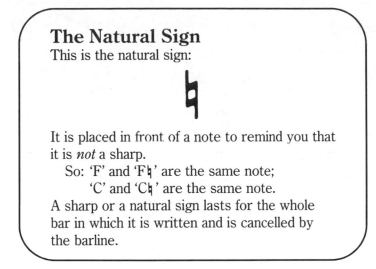

It is placed in front of a note to remind you that it is *not* a sharp.

So: 'F' and 'F♮' are the same note;

'C' and 'C♮' are the same note.

A sharp or a natural sign lasts for the whole bar in which it is written and is cancelled by the barline.

Time for Jazz

J.D.

KEY: G MAJOR
CHECK FINGER PATTERN
ON PAGE 56

Calypso

J.D.

> accent

Winds over Mountain Tops

J.D.

Rounds for Four Players

Magnificent March

Early Morning

Fantastic Fanfare

Tap Dance

A New Position for Second Finger on the G String

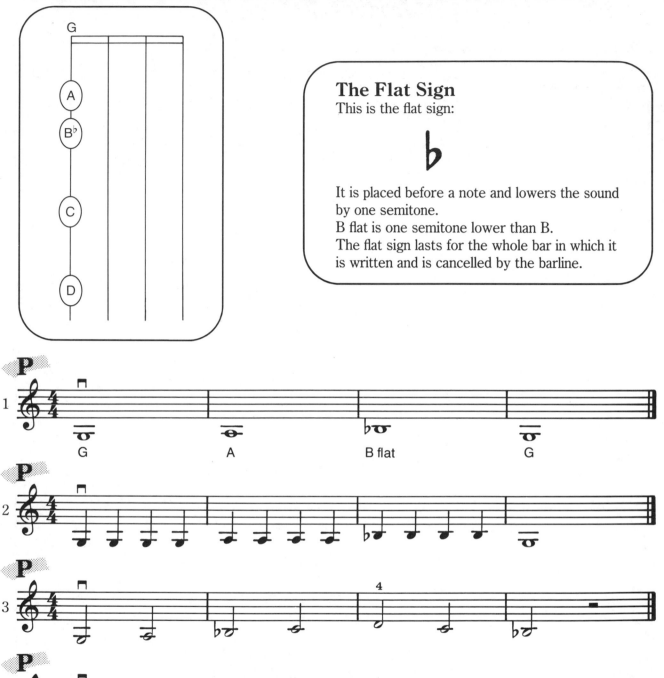

G

A

B♭

C

D

The Flat Sign
This is the flat sign:

♭

It is placed before a note and lowers the sound by one semitone.
B flat is one semitone lower than B.
The flat sign lasts for the whole bar in which it is written and is cancelled by the barline.

1

G   A   B flat   G

2

3

4

4

5 *andante*

Faraway Hills

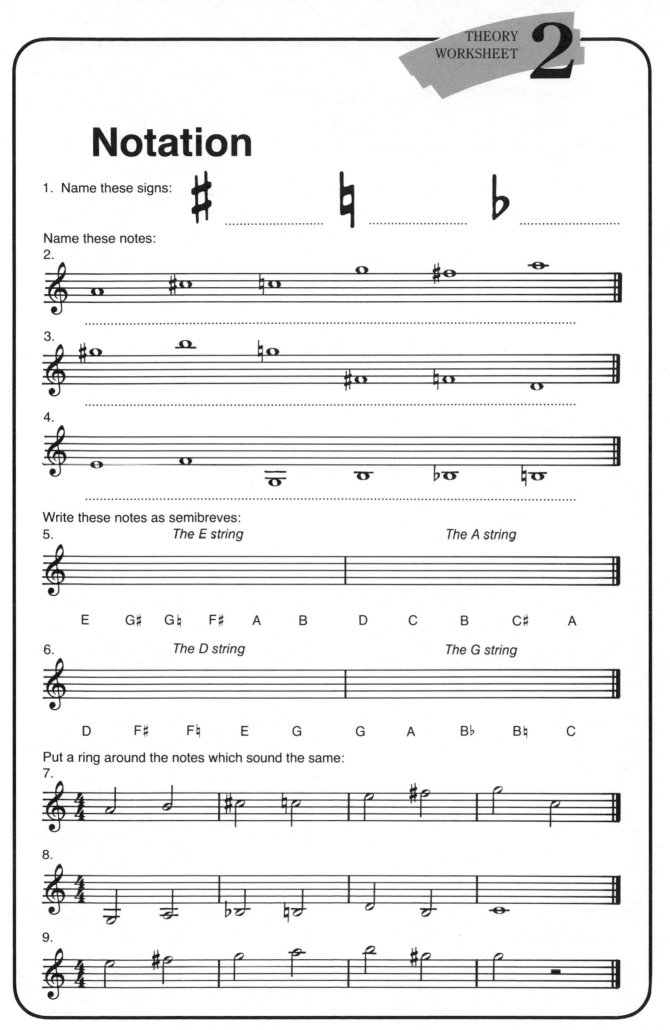

Notation

1. Name these signs: ♯ .... ♮ .... ♭ ....

Name these notes:

2.

....

3.

....

4.

....

Write these notes as semibreves:

5. *The E string*   *The A string*

E   G♯   G♮   F♯   A   B   D   C   B   C♯   A

6. *The D string*   *The G string*

D   F♯   F♮   E   G   G   A   B♭   B♮   C

Put a ring around the notes which sound the same:

7.

8.

9.

SECTION 3

The Dotted Crotchet

When a dot is added to a note it lengthens the note by half its value.

A crotchet ♩ receives *one* count.

A dotted crotchet ♩. receives *one and a half* counts.

In a $\frac{3}{4}$ bar the dotted crotchet lasts for one whole beat and half of the next beat.

Clap these rhythms:

Now clap and play this exercise:

Carol – Trio

Traditional

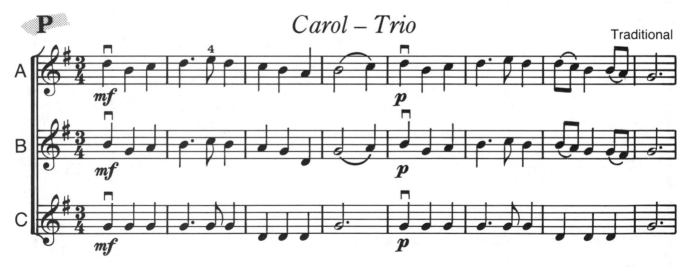

Clap the following rhythms:

1 2 + 3 4   1 2 + 3 4   1 2 + 3 4   1 2 + 3 4

Now clap and play this exercise:

1 2 + 3 4   1 2 + 3 4

Winster Galop – Trio

Traditional

Bowing Exercises

Lifted Bowings

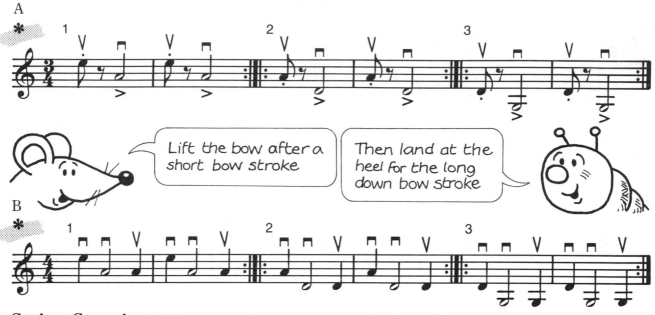

String Crossing (with separate bows or slurred as below)

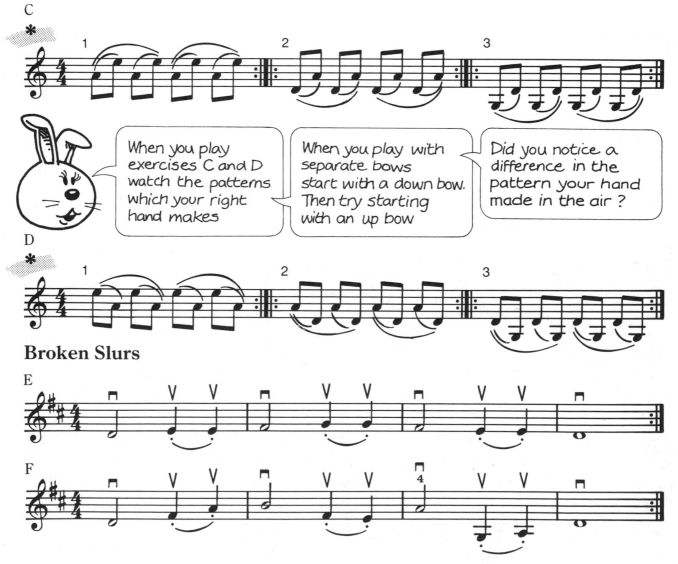

Broken Slurs

Theme and Variations

The Semiquaver

Four semiquavers are the same length as one crotchet:

Two semiquavers are the same length as one quaver:

Clap this rhythm:

> Use these words to help you with the rhythms

♩ = Cheese   ♫ = Edam   ♫♫ = Gorgonzola

= Camembert   = Cream cracker

Play the scale of D major in semiquavers:

Double Stopping (playing two notes at the same time)

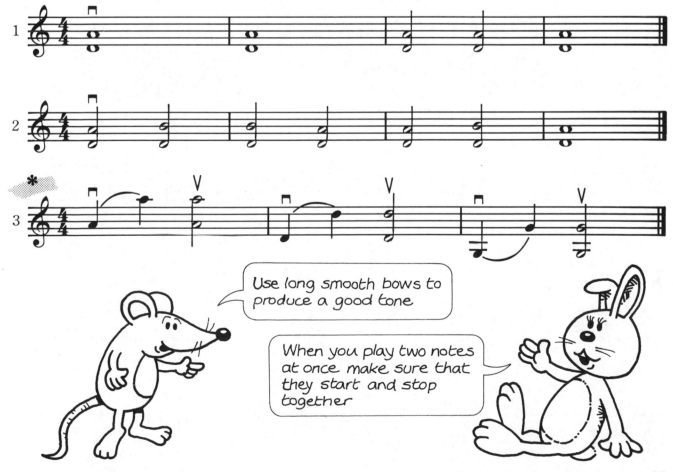

> Use long smooth bows to produce a good tone

> When you play two notes at once make sure that they start and stop together

Some Rhythm Patterns for You to Play

Use them when you practise your scales.

Left Hand Pizzicato

Pluck the notes marked with a cross using your 4th finger

Clever Clogs

A major

 **Time**

6̸/8̸ time means that there are six quavers in each bar.
The quavers are divided into two main beats.

Clap this rhythm. Make the first and fourth quavers louder than the others:

1　2　3　4　5　6
first beat　　second beat

Clap this rhythm:

1　2　3　4　5　6　　1　2　3　4　5　6
Hump - ty Dump - ty　　sat　on　the　wall.

Now play the tune:

Joseph Dearest, Joseph Mine

German, fourteenth century

Oats and Beans

Traditional

Note Values and Rests

Note Values

1. Fill in a note A of the correct value in each of the spaces marked with an asterisk:

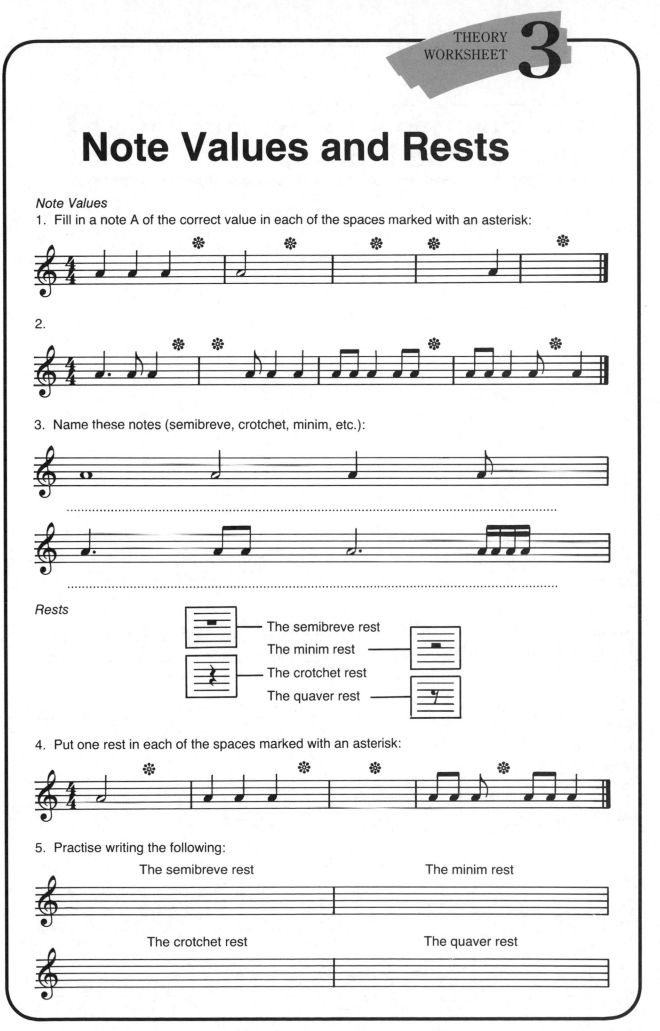

2.

3. Name these notes (semibreve, crotchet, minim, etc.):

Rests

The semibreve rest
The minim rest
The crotchet rest
The quaver rest

4. Put one rest in each of the spaces marked with an asterisk:

5. Practise writing the following:

The semibreve rest   The minim rest

The crotchet rest   The quaver rest

SECTION 4

A New Position for First and Fourth Fingers on the E String

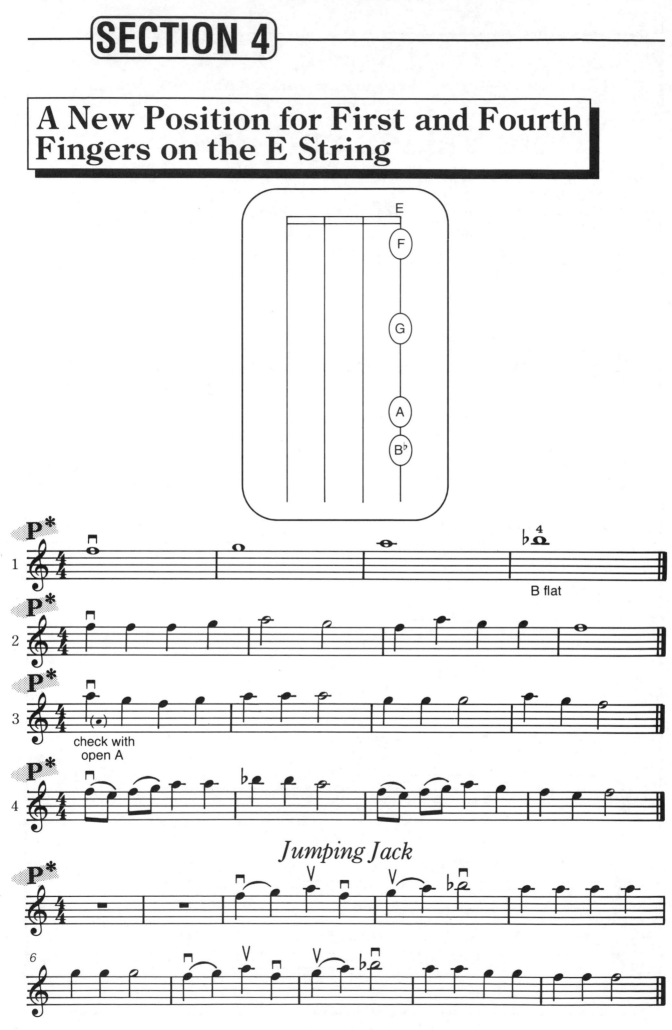

A New Position for First and Fourth Fingers on the A String

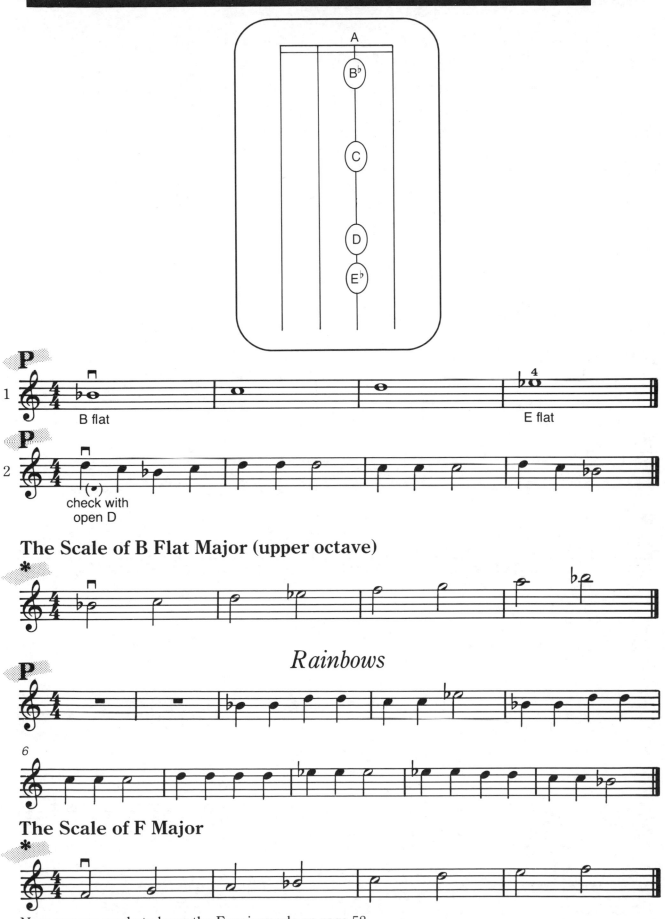

The Scale of B Flat Major (upper octave)

Rainbows

The Scale of F Major

Now you are ready to learn the F major scale on page 58.

A New Position for First and Fourth Fingers on the D String

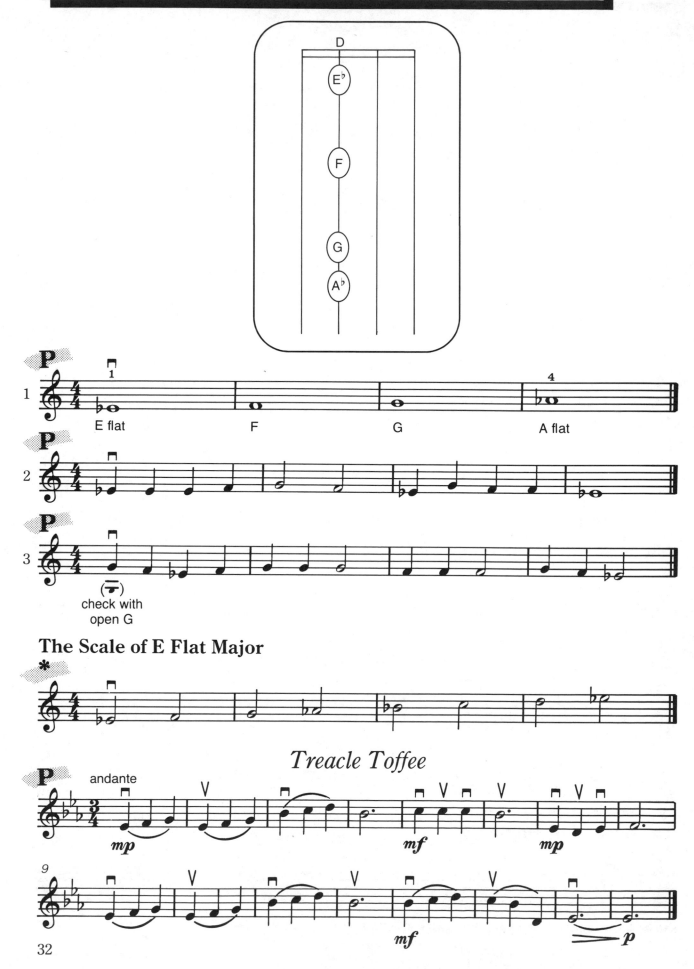

The Scale of E Flat Major

Treacle Toffee

A New Position for First and Fourth Fingers on the G String

A flat   B flat   C   D flat

Zipper-Zapper

Merrily We Roll Along

The Scale of B Flat Major (lower octave)

Now you are ready to learn the scale of B flat major (two octaves) on page 56.

The Triplet

A triplet is formed by writing three notes in the time of two notes:

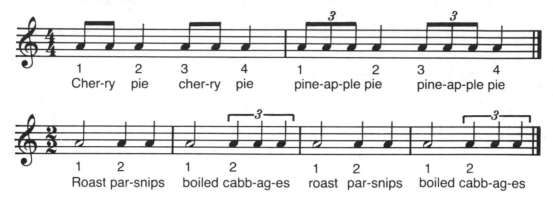

1	2	3	4	1	2	3	4
Cher-ry	pie	cher-ry	pie	pine-ap-ple pie		pine-ap-ple pie	

1	2	1	2	1	2	1	2
Roast par-snips		boiled cabb-ag-es		roast par-snips		boiled cabb-ag-es	

Triplets are grouped together and have a figure 3 written against them.

Bugle Call

Fine

D.C. al Fine

KEY: B FLAT MAJOR
CHECK FINGER PATTERN
ON PAGE 56

Breton Dance – Duet

allegro

Traditional
Fine

A

Fine

B

D.C. al Fine

D.C. al Fine

34

CREATING MUSICAL PICTURES

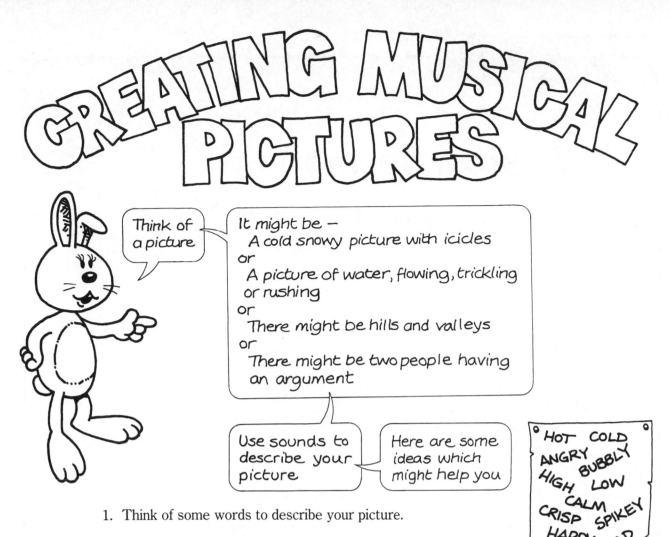

Think of a picture

It might be —
A cold snowy picture with icicles
or
A picture of water, flowing, trickling or rushing
or
There might be hills and valleys
or
There might be two people having an argument

Use sounds to describe your picture

Here are some ideas which might help you

HOT COLD
ANGRY BUBBLY
HIGH LOW
CALM
CRISP SPIKEY
HAPPY SAD

1. Think of some words to describe your picture.

2. The sounds you make can be:

HIGH	LOW
SLOW	FAST

LOUD SOFT

SMOOTH	STACCATO
SHORT	LONG

3. Decide which sounds are best for your picture.

4. Try using

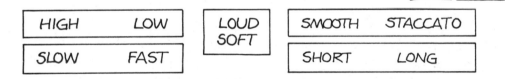

SLURRED BOWING   LIFTED BOWINGS

STACCATO   ACCENTS

PIZZICATO WITH LEFT OR RIGHT HAND

to create the sounds you want.

5. Think about how you could use rhythm patterns in your music:

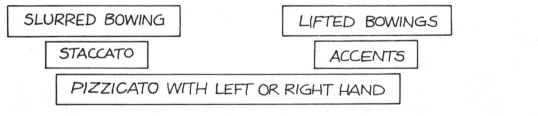

a fast rhythm.

a slow rhythm.

Keep experimenting with sounds until you are pleased with your musical picture

Look at page 26 where there are some more rhythm patterns.

Musical Terms

Draw a line linking each Italian word to the correct English meaning:

1. *allegro*   at a moderate pace
   andante   fairly fast
   lento   loud
   forte (f)   soft
   piano (p)   quick, lively
   allegretto   slow

2. *arco*   moderately loud
   pizzicato   play with the bow
   mezzo-forte (mf)   moderately soft
   mezzo-piano (mp)   pluck the string

3. *crescendo*   gradually slower
   diminuendo   back to the normal speed
   fine   becoming gradually louder
   ritardando   becoming gradually softer
   a tempo   the end

4. *staccato*   very loud
   legato   very soft
   fortissimo (ff)   detached, short
   pianissimo (pp)   smooth

5. Add bowing marks to the following tune, making some notes sound short and detached, and some notes sound smooth and flowing. Play the tune on your violin to help you to decide on the bowing marks.

6. Now decide how fast the tune should go, and how loud or soft each phrase should be. Add the correct signs.

The Harmonic Minor Scale and Arpeggio

In the harmonic minor scale the third and sixth notes are a semitone lower than in the major scale.

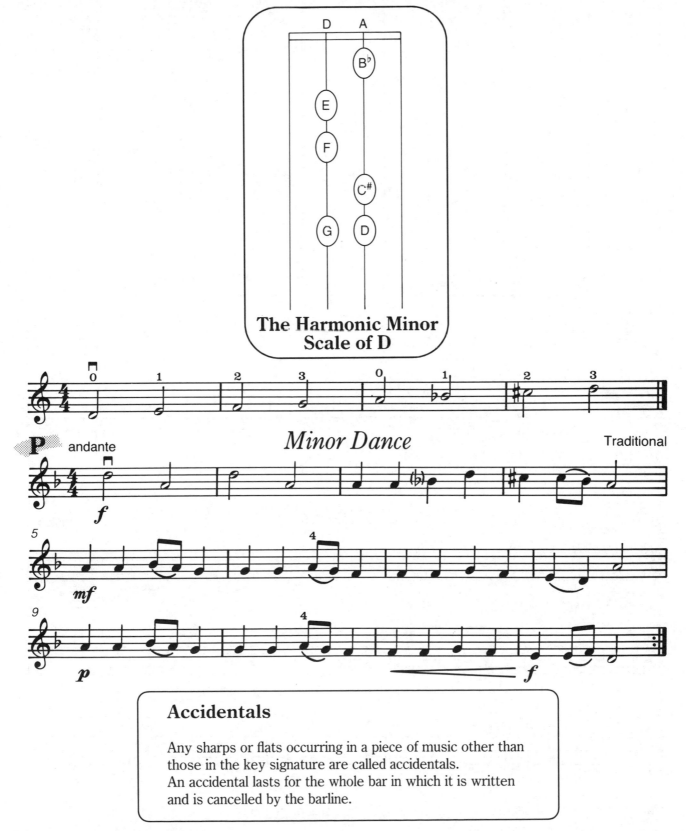

The Harmonic Minor Scale of D

Minor Dance

andante   Traditional

Accidentals

Any sharps or flats occurring in a piece of music other than those in the key signature are called accidentals.
An accidental lasts for the whole bar in which it is written and is cancelled by the barline.

The Melodic Minor Scale of D

In the melodic minor scale the third note is flattened ascending and the third, sixth, and seventh notes are flattened descending.

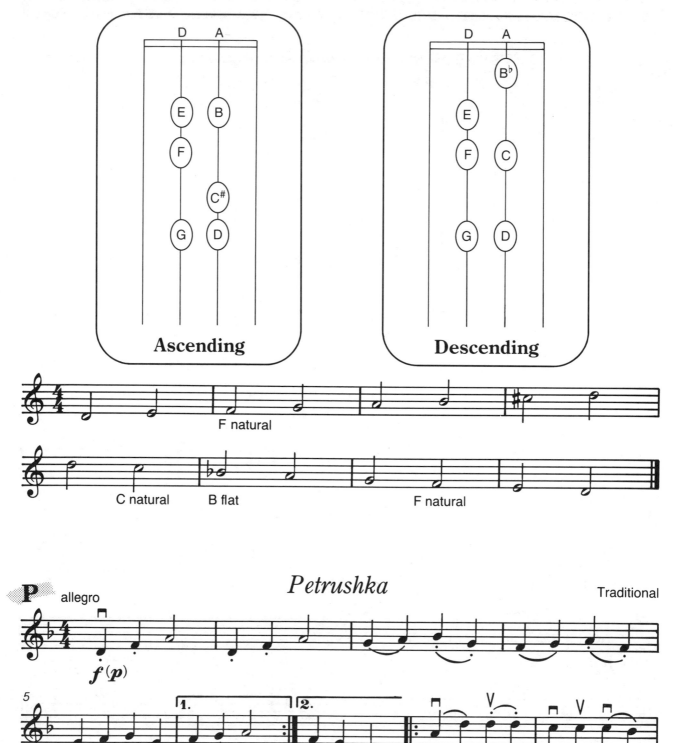

Ascending

Descending

F natural

C natural   B flat   F natural

Petrushka

P allegro

Traditional

f (p)

f

mf

f

Now you are ready to learn the minor scales and arpeggios on page 60.

1. Decide which key you will use and play the scale to remind yourself of the finger pattern.

2. Choose a time signature.

3. Make up a phrase and then follow it with an answering phrase.

4. Try making a longer tune. Can you join four phrases together?

Two Notes with the Same Sound

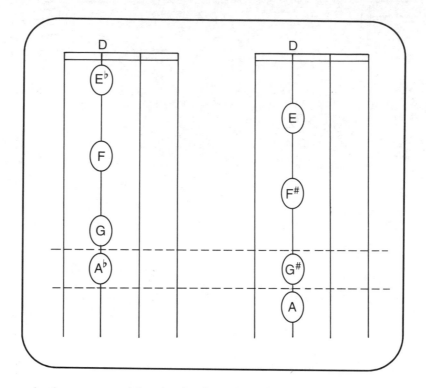

A flat and G sharp are in the same position on the fingerboard and make the same sound.

Monkey Nuts

Two New Third Finger Notes — D Sharp and A Sharp

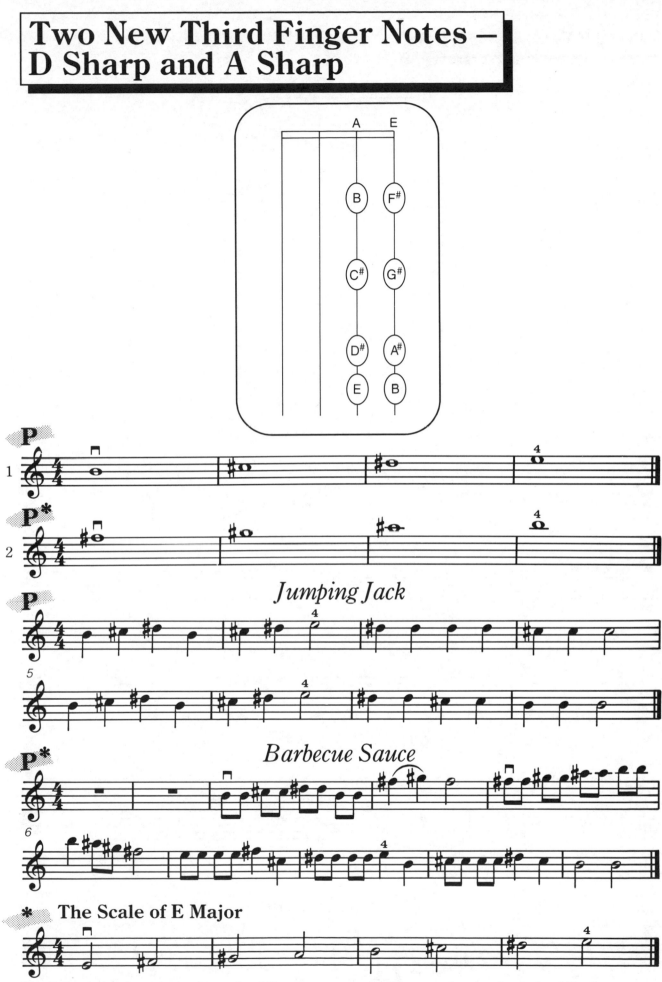

Now you are ready to learn the scale of E major on page 58. You can also try the scale of E minor on page 60.

A New C Sharp

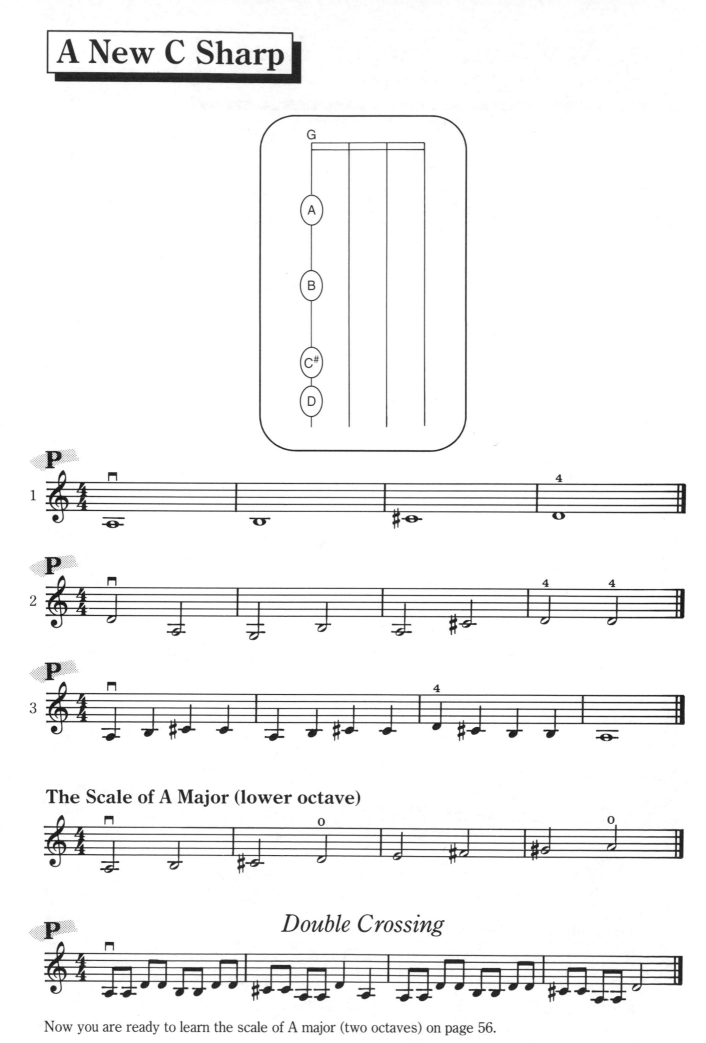

The Scale of A Major (lower octave)

Double Crossing

Now you are ready to learn the scale of A major (two octaves) on page 56.

D major

Weeping Willows

J.D.

A major

Singing Woodcocks

J.D.

E major

Marching Drums

J.D.

Building Tunes Step by Step

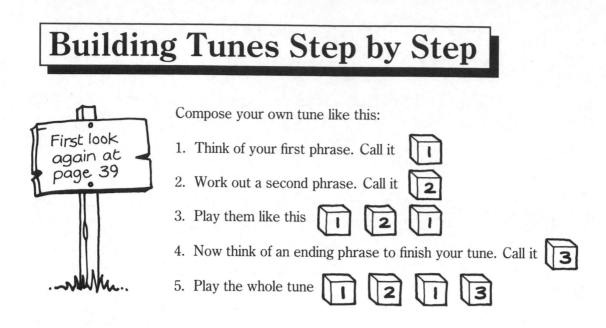

First look again at page 39

Compose your own tune like this:

1. Think of your first phrase. Call it ☐1

2. Work out a second phrase. Call it ☐2

3. Play them like this ☐1 ☐2 ☐1

4. Now think of an ending phrase to finish your tune. Call it ☐3

5. Play the whole tune ☐1 ☐2 ☐1 ☐3

Composing Longer Tunes

Many composers join two tunes together to make a longer tune. If the first tune is called TUNE A and the second TUNE B the pattern they make might look like this:

Here is a traditional dance tune with the pattern TUNE A, TUNE B. Can you spot the four phrases in each tune?

Sometimes tunes have the pattern A B A.
Listen to 'Humming Song' by Schumann which has this pattern.
Whenever you play a new tune try to spot the phrases and the patterns which they make.

Key Chart

MAJOR KEYS	KEY SIGNATURES	MINOR KEYS	ACCIDENTALS IN MINOR KEYS
C major	No sharp or flats	A minor	G♯
G major	F♯	E minor	D♯
D major	F♯ C♯		
A major	F♯ C♯ G♯		
E major	F♯ C♯ G♯ D♯		
F major	B♭	D minor	C♯
B flat major	B♭ E♭	G minor	F♯
E flat major	B♭ E♭ A♭		

Minor Keys

The raised seventh note which forms a semitone between the seventh and eighth notes in the harmonic minor scale is called an accidental and does not appear in the key signature.

A minor key has the same key signature as the major scale which starts three semitones above it.

This is the harmonic minor scale starting on D. It has the same key signature as F major and the accidental is C♯, the seventh note. It is RELATIVE to F major because it has the same key signature.

so . . . E minor is *relative* to G major;
       A minor is *relative* to C major;
       D minor is *relative* to F major.

Major Keys

Add the correct key signature in the spaces marked with an asterisk:

1. G major

2. D major

3. A major

4. E major

Name the keys of these tunes and write the key signature in the blank stave:

5.

Key name ....

6.

Key name ....

7.

Key name ....

8.

Key name ....

SECTION 6

J'irai Revoir ma Normandie – Trio

Traditional

Basque Song – Trio

Traditional

Performance Suggestions

First Time:
 All play A.
Second Time:
 Play in three parts.

With violas and cellos:
 Violins play A;
 Violas play B;
 Cellos play C.

N.B. You may like to vary the
order to suit yourself.

Dotted Quavers and Semiquavers

A dotted quaver is equal to three semiquavers or three quarters of a crotchet beat.

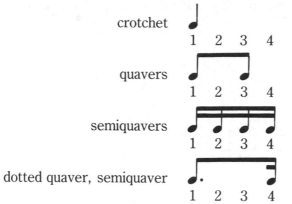

Clap these rhythms:

Time Signatures

Add the time signatures to these tunes:

Write a short rhythm on one note or a tune using the time signatures given below:

5.

6.

7.

8.

SIGHT-READING

Sing these tunes:

Clap these rhythms:

Play these tunes:

Look at the key and prepare your finger shape.

Major keys

Minor keys

Major Scales and Arpeggios (One Octave)

G major

G   D

⊓   V   ⊓   V   ⊓

0 – 1 – 2 3 – 0 – 1 – 2 3

D major

D   A

⊓   V   ⊓   V   ⊓

0 – 1 – 2 3 – 0 – 1 – 2 3

A major

A   E

⊓   V   ⊓   V   ⊓

0 – 1 – 2 3 – 0 – 1 – 2 3

Arpeggios

G major

0 2 0 3

D major

0 2 0 3

A major

0 2 0 3

Finger Patterns for the Scales

G major

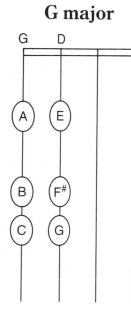

D major

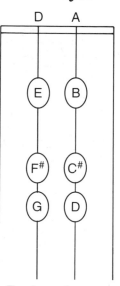

For key shape on
other strings see
pages 14 and 42.

A major

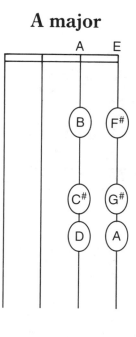

Scales

G major

D major

A major

Arpeggios

G major

D major

A major

Major Scales and Arpeggios (Two Octaves)

G major

```
G              D              A              E
⊓  V  ⊓     V  ⊓  V     ⊓     V     ⊓
0 – 1 – 2 3 – 0 – 1 – 2 3 – 0 – 1 2 – 3 – 0 – 1 2
```

A major

```
G           D              A           E
⊓  V  ⊓     V  ⊓  V     ⊓     V     ⊓
1 – 2 – 3 0 – 1 – 2 – 3 0 – 1 – 2 3 – 0 – 1 – 2 3
```

B flat major

```
G     D              A              E
⊓  V  ⊓     V        ⊓  V     ⊓     V     ⊓
2 – 3 – 0 1 – 2 – 3 – 0 1 – 2 – 3 4 – 1 – 2 – 3 4
low
```

Arpeggios

G major

```
⊓        V
0 2 0 3 1 3 2
⊓     V     ⊓
```

A major

```
⊓        V
1 3 1 0 2 0 3
⊓     V     ⊓
```

B flat major

```
⊓        V
2 0 2 1 3 1 4
⊓     V     ⊓
```

Finger Patterns for the Scales

G major

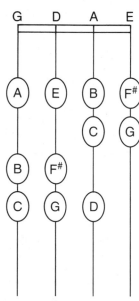

A major

B flat major

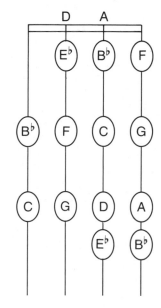

For key shape on
E string see page 14.

56

Scales

G major

A major

B flat major

Arpeggios

G major

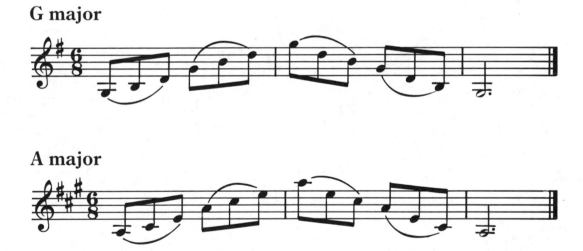

A major

B flat major

Some More Major Scales and Arpeggios (One Octave)

C major

Arpeggios

```
G   D           A
⊓   V   ⊓       V   ⊓
3 - 0 - 1 2 - 3 - 0 - 1 2
```

3 1 3 2

F major

```
D       A           E
⊓   V   ⊓       V   ⊓
2 - 3 - 0 1 - 2 - 3 - 0 1
low
```

2 0 2 1

E major

```
D       A
⊓   V   ⊓   V   ⊓
1 - 2 - 3 4 - 1 - 2 - 3 4
```

```
⊓       V
1 3 1 4
```

E flat major

```
D       A
⊓   V   ⊓   V   ⊓
1 - 2 - 3 4 - 1 - 2 - 3 4
low
```

```
⊓       V
1 3 1 4
```

Finger Patterns for the Scales

C major	F major	E major	E flat major

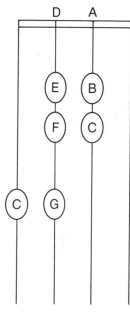

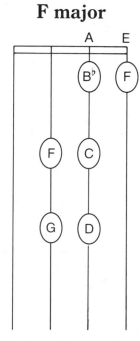

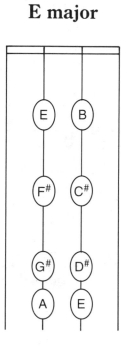

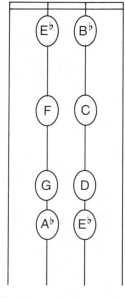

For key shape on E string see pattern on page 30 (excluding fourth finger).

For key shape on G and E strings see pages 18 and 30.

For key shape on G string see page 33 (excluding D flat).

Scales

C major

F major

E major

E flat major

Arpeggios

C major

F major

E major

E flat major

Harmonic Minor Scales (One Octave)

G, D, and A minors

⊓ V ⊓ V ⊓

0 – 1 2 – 3 – 0 1 – – 2 3

0 2 0 3
low

E minor

D   A

⊓ V ⊓ V ⊓

1 – 2 3 – 4 – 1 2 – – 3 4

⊓ V

1 3 1 4

Finger Patterns for the Scales

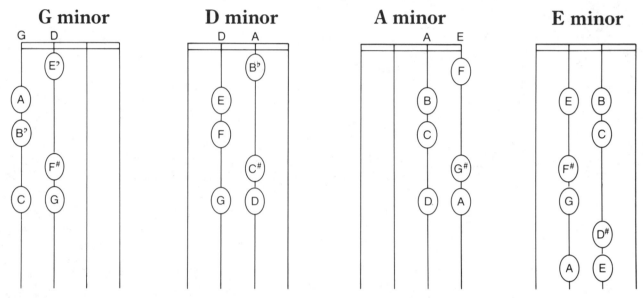

G minor   **D minor**   **A minor**   **E minor**

Melodic Minor Scales (One Octave)

G, D, and A minors

0 – 1 2 – 3 – 0 – 1 – 2 3 – 2 – 1 0 – 3 – 2 1 – 0

E minor

D   A   D

1 – 2 3 – 4 – 1 – 2 – 3 4 – 3 – 2 1 – 4 – 3 2 – 1

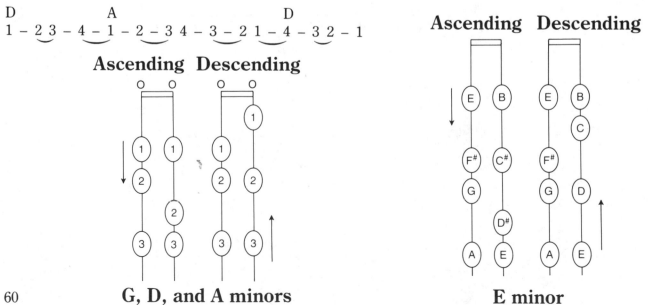

Ascending   **Descending**

Ascending   **Descending**

     G, D, and A minors   **E minor**

Scales

G minor (harmonic)

G minor (melodic)

D minor (harmonic)

D minor (melodic)

A minor (harmonic)

A minor (melodic)

E minor (harmonic)

E minor (melodic)

Arpeggios

G minor

D minor

A minor

E minor

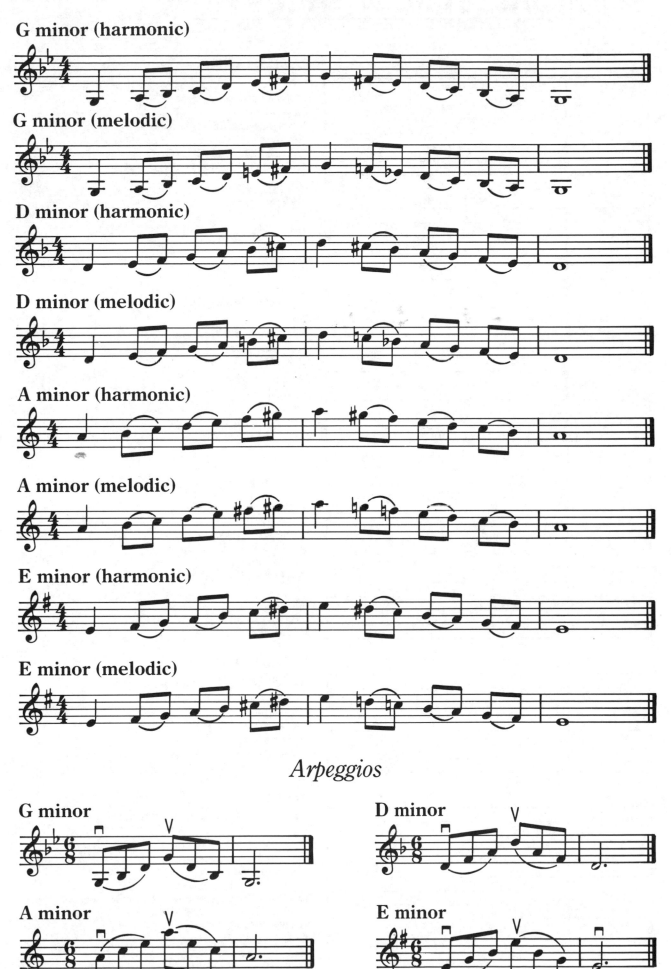

ACHIEVEMENT RECORD

Section 1

Page	√	Comment
6		
7		
9		
9		
10		
11		

Revision Exercises
Scale Games
'When the Saints Come Marching In'
'Kumbaya'
'O Come Little Children' – Trio
Improvisation – Answering Phrases

Section 2

Page	√	Comment
12		
13		
14		
15		
15		
16		
16		
17		
18		

The D String
The A String
The E String
The Natural Sign
'Time for Jazz'
'Calypso'
'Winds over Mountain Tops'
Rounds
The G String. The Flat Sign.

Section 3

Page	√	Comment
20		
20		
21		
22		
22		
22		
22		
22		
22		
23		
23		
24		
25		
26		
27		
27		
28		
28		
28		

The Dotted Crotchet
'Carol' – Trio
'Winster Galop' – Trio
Bowing Exercises – A
B
C
D
E
F
'Hoop-La'
'Catherine Wheels'
'Theme and Variations'
The Semiquaver. Double Stopping.
Rhythm Patterns
'Wild Geese'
'Theme'
6/8 Time
'Joseph Dearest'
'Oats and Beans'

Section 4

Page	√	Comment
30		
31		
32		
33		
34		
34		
35		

The E String
The A String
The D String
The G String
The Triplet
'Breton Dance' – Duet
Creating Musical Pictures

Section 5

Page	√	Comment
37		
37		
38		
38		
39		
40		
41		
42		
43		
43		
43		
44		

The Harmonic Minor Scale of D. Accidentals.
'Minor Dance'
The Melodic Minor Scale of D
'Petrushka'
Inventing a Tune
Two Notes with the Same Sound
Two New Third Finger Notes – D Sharp and A Sharp
A New C Sharp
'Weeping Willows'
'Singing Woodcocks'
'Marching Drums'
Building Tunes Step by Step

Performance Plan 1

....
....
....
....
....
....

Performance Plan 2

....
....
....
....
....
....

Performance Plan 3

....
....
....
....
....
....

Comments on Posture and Style

	SECTION 1 SECTION 2	SECTION 3 SECTION 4	SECTION 5 SECTION 6
LEFT HAND			
BOWING			
POSTURE			

Theory Worksheets

	√	Comment
WORKSHEET 1 – REVISION		
WORKSHEET 2 – NOTATION		
WORKSHEET 3 – NOTE VALUES AND RESTS		
WORKSHEET 4 – MUSICAL TERMS		
WORKSHEET 5 – MAJOR KEYS		
WORKSHEET 6 – TIME SIGNATURES		

Overall Assessment

POSTURE AND STYLE	
SCALES	
ARPEGGIOS	
EXERCISES	
SOLO PIECES	
ENSEMBLES	
AURAL	
IMPROVISATION	
GENERAL COMMENT	